T0373993

Over the Rainbow

Joanne Lily Kendall

Autobiography

To order additional copies of this book, contact:
Xlibris
0800-056-3182
www.xlibrispublishing.co.uk
Orders@ Xlibrispublishing.co.uk

Over the Rainbow

Joanne Lily Kendall

A big THANKYOU
to Marie Barrett for her dedicated help
to June and Ray Thompson, Mary, Brian, Maxine and Seventh Day
Adventist friends and Keith Brown for their helpful inspirations.

THANKYOU to my two daughters, Karen and Sandralee. Also Alan and Gill.
Kath J., Gillian E., Jean F., Pat T., Cynthia F., Friends in Art. Beverley S
and Just Good Friends, Dorothy B. Cameo Club, Jackie B, Jon H, Arlene
R and Penny H, and all my grandchildren another big THANKYOU.

Prologue

Looking back, so many questions come to mind. Why did this happen? It had nothing to do with politics, only my own life. My mother and I were saved at the beginning of World War II by not travelling on the ship which was torpedoed on its way to Canada in the year 1940. The reason was that I had heart trouble. Of course, the war carried on until 1945. There were so many happenings about being bombed out three times and saved twice.

In 1945 many, many children were evacuated from Morden, Surrey; I was evacuated to North Wales. This was because the Germans threatened to drop gas bombs. But I should begin at the very beginning.

My dad called me Joanee. My mother called me Jo. In the 1930s, I was christened Joanne Lily Wright, but a lot of people shortened my name to Joan. Yes, that's right, my surname was Wright; the olden name was Wheelwright. The Wheelwrights, my paternal ancestors, joined an Irish coach-building firm who made the royal carriages being used today. It is not generally known, but the men standing on the lid at the back of the carriage when the carriage is being used by the royal family, are the great-grandchildren of the coach-makers and they are called livery men.

Many events transpired, so to begin, see the following chapters.

CHAPTER ONE

Early Years

Edward, Prince of Wales (future King Edward VIII), patron of Lady Drummond-Hay's circle, was attending her garden party. At the same party, my mother and I were present. Edward took me in his arms, kissed me on the cheek, tickled me under the chin, and on handing me back to my mother, told her that I would be successful—so my mother told me. At that time, I was about fourteen months old. I was a pretty baby with little near-white curls—so I've been told—and, yes, also big blue eyes which had teardrops in them, so apparently, I always got my way. It's hearsay, but it is possibly true (because I do that now too).

My mother had been Edward's ex–dancing partner when she was head girl in a Cornish convent four years previous, when they held a dance festival. So at the garden party, he noticed my mother and was surprised to see her nursing a baby (me).

Lady Drummond-Hay was my godmother, and her garden parties were awesome. She held a garden party every year until she was called up to join the Ambulance Service. She was a fine lady, and her significant work has been encapsulated in her memoirs.

Lady Drummond-Hay had many godchildren; she adopted them as godchildren if they were born in her ward in St George Hospital, Knightsbridge (where the luxurious Lanesborough Hotel now stands). If an expectant mother spent more than three weeks in her ward, Lady Drummond-Hay would ask to be godmother to the new baby. She loved children.

During the war (1939 to 1945), we lived in Morden, Surrey (near Wimbledon). I remember looking out of my bedroom window and seeing the whole panoramic view on fire; streets of houses were falling down around us. We were bombed three times, and the noise from the guns being fired was so loud and horrendous. If a house did not fall down, often the windows were blown in, and the front and back doors were torn off their hinges. After a raid, no house stood intact.

Many people who lived in London during the war had their sleeping accommodation on the platforms of every underground station. In fact, my future husband was one of the children from Baker Street, London, living in two places—at home or in the underground, with his mother, father, and aunties. Whole families lived in the underground. Every time the air-raid warning sounded, the street became alive with people running to the nearest underground station or air-raid shelter. Classes were often cancelled because everyone was down in the shelters or sometimes because the school had been bombed.

In those days, everyone helped each other, wearing each other's clothes and handing around different furniture to move into different addresses. Most men were in the forces, and young girls and mothers worked in factories or in the Land Army.

My mother worked in the Lines Bros factory in Wimbledon, Surrey, where they made Sten guns and army ammunition since the beginning of and throughout the war years. Before the war, they made Dinky Toys, Hornby train sets, Pedigree prams, and also the first large talking dolls. No, I never had one, or a Pedigree pram; they were far too expensive for my mum and dad to buy.

My mother was Mr Bob Lines' personal assistant during the war years. Previously, when working on the factory floor, she had been injured, so he was keeping an eye on her to ensure she would not be hurt again. He thought it safer that way!

The Lines firm started from these humble beginnings and it was a real achievement to have progressed to such heights after their great-grandfather's first task of wearing a tray round his neck, selling boxes of matches, and then making matchbox toys. The factory in Wimbledon was huge.

The following episode was the beginning of what can be termed an eventful life for me. SS *City of Benares* was torpedoed by the Germans in 1940 on its way to Canada. My mother and I were detailed to climb aboard, but we were refused because I had whooping cough and pleurisy, which had caused a hole in my heart. This was not good news since we were keen to get away from Wimbledon, where the Germans bombarded us with bombs. We lived in the danger zone. However, tragedy occurred; 260 of the 407 crew and passengers on the *Benares* were lost, including most of the children, when the ship was torpedoed.

My dad a young soldier WW1

My father was in the Army, stationed in Scotland. His job was to manage a radar light to scan the sky. Radar was quite a new invention. Unfortunately he was injured and hospitalised when he was hit in the back by the backlash of a big gun.

The war was a terrible time for everybody. In the beginning, young men were taken away from their studies to go and fight for our country. Our food was scarce and rationed. In some areas, there was little choice of food to buy. Most delicious items, like oranges and bananas, were not available. Also, eggs were scarce, so powdered eggs were brought in to make tasteless scrambled egg on toast. So my mother told me.

When I was little, I attended a wedding in Lambeth, London. I heard a noise, so I investigated outside the front door, ran up nine floors on to the roof, and ran into a bombardment of incendiary bombs, horrible big black tin-like things falling on the roof and causing fires. Being really scared, I ran to the edge and wanted to jump off the roof, when my uncle grabbed me and carried me back downstairs to safety. This tenement building was nine storeys high, so it would have been a long fall for me. The Germans dropped Butterfly Bombs too, one of the first cluster bombs, but the British people did not complain openly, so the Germans couldn't guess how terrible the bombs were. They were nicknamed Butterfly Bombs because they gave the appearance of a large butterfly falling from the sky, and were the worst things ever invented.

This incident on the roof, was the second miracle of my life, the first miracle being when I was refused permission to sail on the torpedoed SS *Benares*, due to heart trouble.

My father's mother was Lily Shepherd, know as Nannie to my cousin Audrey and me. Lily had two brothers and one sister, Amy. Amy married Hermann Carl Reuter, whose grandfather was well known in the telegraph business. My father's cousin was Montague Fawcett Phillips, who is well known in the music world for having written an opera called *The Rebel Maid*. A popular song from that opera is 'The Fishermen of England'. He wrote several orchestral pieces and married Clara Butterworth, a noted opera singer.

My father grew up surrounded by talent, but tragedy befell him when he was struck with polio at age twelve. At age eighteen, he was suddenly enlisted in the First World War during its last year of horror.

Nannie adopted a young girl named Lillian Sewell, who was known to me as Auntie Lillian. She became my second godmother, and on Sundays she took me to St Leonard's Church, Streatham, where my dad played the bells in the tower. Every Sunday, I would trundle up the spiral staircase to sit and watch the bell-ringers standing in a circle, all pulling coloured ropes. My dad pulled the No. 10 bell, which was the heaviest.

During the day, my Auntie Lillian was a royal court dressmaker; she used to go to the palace to measure the two princesses. She always made four matching dresses, one each for Princesses Elizabeth and Margaret Rose, my cousin Audrey, and me. One day I couldn't find one dress, and my mother told me she had to give it back to Auntie Lillian because it was chosen by the Princess to wear in a royal photograph. After that, my auntie didn't make any more dresses for Audrey and me.

The war was still raging in 1942. All British people wanted it to finish but the bombs were still falling, and then the Germans decided to up the devastation by sending over V-2 bombs, which were unlike a buzz bomb (which was smaller but still able to destroy properties). The difference was the fact that the V-2 destroyed a whole street, and other surrounding houses lost windows, roofs, and doors. There were not many V-2s because again the British people did not openly cause a big fuss, but one bomb alone did a lot of damage to our house.

My parents' wedding day, 1931.

My parents had already gone into our garden Anderson (tin) shelter; each thought I had already arrived. Unfortunately, I wasn't well and was still in my bed, which was downstairs, when a V-2 fell. The blast lifted me up, and I was pushed under the bed.

The kettle, which was on a trivet in a coal fire, was also lifted up, and hot water spilled over, burning my arm.

Eventually, my parents came running into the house and called out for me. They saw me under the bed, which was a steel bed, so they called for the fire brigade to help. They used a blowtorch, and eventually I was lifted out. I had to go to St Helier Hospital, mainly because my arm was burned.

Unfortunately, a few days later, a buzz bomb fell nearby just when I was walking down our stairs. The blast threw me sideways, and I got my head stuck in the staircase. The same firemen came to saw me free, and unlike me, they saw the funny side of it.

My third miracle occurred when a twelve-year-old girl who was looking after me, hid by an oak tree in our park when a buzz bomb fell and split our tree down the middle. She was blown to pieces; I only had her hand, and our bike spokes were all round me. In hospital, the staff took ages to take away the spokes. My friend was lovely; that should never have happened.

Our local hospital was called St Helier's. When Queen Mary came to lay the first stone a little girl of three shouted out, 'That's not a queen. That's a grandma!' 'Never a truer word,' a man said to my mother. (I wonder who the rude little girl was!) Queen Mary had been dressed all in black, with a big flat black hat—nothing like a little girl's idea of a queen. They drove in a horrible big black car; the queen was all in black. I thought I was going to see a queen all dressed up in a big pretty dress. Ah, well – it was only a little girl's thoughts.

Unfortunately, there was a fourth miracle. It involved five children being buried in a shelter from Tuesday to Sunday, the only survivors of a vast bombing. Being small, I didn't know that little Jimmy Wright, lying across my lap, was not alive. I thought

he was asleep. The five of us had a big jar of barley sugars and a crate of bottles of pop. On Sunday, after hearing a big noise above us, a hole appeared, and we five were found. All of us were taken to hospital. It was a miracle for my Mum because she had been walking back to our shelter, which was hit. She was blown sky-high and was in a coma in hospital for sixteen days. She eventually came to.

My father had been sent home on compassionate leave to bury my mother and me but when he went to the hospital, he could not find us in the morgue. A nurse said, 'Come with me, I have a surprise for you. I think we have your daughter.' Well, of course, it was me, and you can imagine his joy. I even remember him crying. Then we heard a noise outside and my mother was brought into my ward in her bed, which they set beside mine. My father and I sat by my mother's bed for many days, until she woke up.

At that time, we had lost our third house, so there was no home to go back to. The St Helier Hospital staff took care of my mother and me until my father found us another house to move into. In all this time, we had a cat called Snowball, and ironically, wherever we went to live, he always found us. When buzz bombs were on their way, Snowball would go and hide under the stairs. This always gave us the clue to go to a nearby shelter even before the siren sounded, alerting everyone else to go to a shelter too. Even dogs had the same instinct and were known to be the savers of lives by alerting owners that an air-raid warning was about to be sounded and giving them enough time to go to safety.

Many films are made depicting the last war, and I avoid every film because I can only cringe at the thought of watching the devastation and horror which we all went through. It was so unbelievably frightening, and I still suffer from nightmares of all the things that happened around me.

At the near end of the war, because the Germans stated that they were going to send over gas bombs, I was suddenly rushed off to North Wales as an evacuee. It was a daunting experience; we had our name on a neck-ribbon and were herded on to a huge train—only little children, no adults. Everyone was crying goodbyes on the platform. On arriving in Flint, North Wales, we were huddled into a big hall. People came in and chose children to take home. One lady, a Mrs Whitehouse, took my two girlfriends, so I started crying. Then when I looked round, everyone had gone; the whole place was empty, except for me and a lady in uniform. Then the door opened, and Mrs Whitehouse burst in and said, 'All right, I'll take her.' She then looked at me and said, 'You three will have to sleep together.'

Staying with Mrs Whitehouse was a lesson in itself. The toilet was in the backyard. Also, we washed in the backyard in a tall round tin drum, and when it was frosty, we had to break the ice to wash. I don't remember starving, so our meals were probably all right. At home, I wasn't allowed to do housework due to me having heart trouble, but no one told Mrs Whitehouse about me, and my condition in particular. I remember one day she sent me to the downstairs shop to buy a jar of elbow grease. I had no idea how to do housework. The most I ever did at any house we lived in was to rub Brasso on the door knocker.

Going to school in Wales was different. All the children had loads of books to read and writing paper, and it was lovely to join the classes. There was a big house near to us where our two boy friends lived, so we three girls went round there often. The ladies gave us ice cream, and we thought they were so rich. Also, sometimes we had cake too.

In school, we made a lot of friends who we all kept in touch with after the war. Everyone was so kind to us, especially the teachers. After five and a half months, the end of the war was declared, and it was not long before my mother travelled to Flint to take me, my two girlfriends, and our two boy friends home. Even so, there were a lot of tearful goodbyes, with promises to visit again, which a lot of us still do.

This time I went back to the same house I had said goodbye in, except my father was not at home. He was in hospital in Tring near Aylesbury, Buckinghamshire. I was surprised when I met him; he was dressed in a light-peacock-blue suit and had a red tie. If he had been on his own dressed like that, it would have been funny, but all the wounded soldiers were dressed the same. He was transferred to Salisbury Hospital, where hundreds of American soldiers were walking around, all holding pretty girls' hands. Back in Morden, there were no American soldiers. The Americans stayed in England a long time after the war. I know a few decided to stay. After all, despite all the bombs, we still had a lovely country to be proud of.

There were VE parties (Victory in Europe) everywhere, in every street, around 8 May 1945, to celebrate the end of the war. Nearly every street was lined with long tables and chairs and what looked like a lot of food. But most of the food was brought to the table by each household for us to eat. We did share.

There was so much noise. Whistles were being blown, balloons were everywhere, and there were whoops of laughter. Everyone was so happy the war was over. It was a day to remember—always. Children and older people all went crazy, kissing everyone in sight and dancing into the early hours.

After a while, when my father was better, we had to try to begin new lives. Even though I was young, I knew it wasn't easy. So many men never returned, so there was a lot of unhappiness around too.

School was horrible. Most children then hated school because there seemed to be nothing to learn. The teachers were all old and more spiteful than they are today. My friends and I were always getting the cane—sitting in a corridor in a row with our hands out while the headmaster walked down the line, giving us a crack on each hand. Ugh. Also, we had few school props, like writing paper and books. Paper and books were in short supply. Of course, this is the time to say we were naughty. It seemed to be more fun to be naughty than good, because we would be sent out into the playground, where we could go scrumping in the back gardens of the surrounding houses, mostly picking apples. People never caught us because the owners were working or the houses were empty and derelict from the falling bombs.

Also, I often caused a rumpus because I would see my boy friends (from the adjoining boys' school) waving at me to join them. It wouldn't take long for me to be sent out to sit in the corridor, which I tried not to do. My mission was to join the boys to go scrumping. (Last time I did any scrumping was on holiday with my boyfriend, Ron Taylor. Naughty us. But that news is too current to mention now.)

As far as I remember, my school days were uneventful. Since I was so naughty on purpose, I learned nothing. I used to mess around in cookery class too. I feel sorry about that, because my cookery teacher was my favourite teacher. But because I was so naughty, my days (after the school was rebuilt) were spent in the secretary's side office, drawing and painting, which ironically got me a scholarship for art. It was even more outstanding because I was the only student who passed the art scholarship, out of 500 girls. In those days, I wanted to have a career in pottery, photography, and textile design, but no such luck. At age fourteen, I left school. My parents would not let me travel to London on the Underground to Regent Street Polytechnic. Wimbledon Polytechnic had been bombed. But Wimbledon Pitmans College in Alwyn Road hadn't been, so my scholarship grant was spent in Pitmans College, in Wimbledon, and eventually in London, learning shorthand, typing, and bookkeeping.

As it happened, after six months, I was sent to London on a course, and my parents had to let me go when I craftily set myself in Pitmans Holborn night school and took a job in London, telling my parents, 'What a good idea. Now I can give you some money, Mum' (which I did). My first wage was spent taking us to the pictures in the 'one and nine pennies'. That was all it cost to see a picture. But my dad had to buy the ice creams because I had run out of money.

After the training course for Pitmans, it was easy for me to transfer to evening classes. I was now used to underground travel. I joined a temporary unit and went from job to job, two weeks each, learning so much.

CHAPTER TWO

Edinburgh - age 15

While studying shorthand, typing and bookkeeping at Pitmans College, London, I worked for The Bank of China. Then another bank - later joined the Bank of British West Africa in Gracechurch Street in the City of London. In those days it was easy to job hop. If a job wasn't suitable the employee would just walk out and a few hours later be working elsewhere. It was that easy.

I made friends with a girl called Valerie who used to stay at my house most weekends. One Friday night we both decided to travel to the Great North Road to hitch a ride to Scotland / keeping it a secret from my Mum and Dad - mistakenly thinking that would be fun. We hitched a lift to Glasgow and was transferred by the driver to his friend going to Edinburgh. On reaching our destination we found a YMCA hostel and booked in for two nights.

Next day we ran wild running up the hill to Edinburgh castle - inside the grounds where the scenery was outstanding because we were so high up. There were huge cannons in the grounds. A flag was flying full mast too, which meant the royal family were present.

The Royal mile (plus 107 yards) walk begins from the gates of Edinburgh Castle to the gates of Holyrood Palace. The Royal Mile has a massive historic history which is really worth delving into since it is so interesting and is a stunning story. Beginning at 325 million years ago depicting the ice age and relating 7000 years ago where people lived in wooden shack houses.

Princess Street, Edinburgh hosted grand shops and was fun just window shopping. Trouble was I only had 10 shillings and 6 pence. Valerie had a little bit more, so we were able to eat snacks.

I decided I wanted to see the Trossachs, a mountain range. We took a bus to the area. Unfortunately we missed the last bus back to Edinburgh, but a doctor offered us a lift to Edinburgh but he suddenly had an idea he wanted a kiss from Valerie - she was 2 years older than me. She refused so he asked me. I refused too, when suddenly he sped his car away from Edinburgh and tipped us out of his car. A horse and cart driver sat us on the back of his cart to his farm —— when we had to walk again. Dropping us on a dirt track, we had to climb a fence - when doing this I fell on top of a sitting cow, then fell sideways into his just left newly pact……not funny, it smelled terrible. Valerie who was taller and bigger than me was having a difficult time climbing the fence. She fell into a field and began walking in cow dung too. We walked for miles until eventually we arrived in Edinburgh near the YMCA, which was locked. We talked to a policeman in his roadside police box - who made us a cup of tea and shared his biscuits. In his box he had a radio and an armchair. He had a comfortable job. He sent us to the local police station where we were locked up in a cell for the night. I gave my real name and suffered a hurt ankle which Valerie did, while she was whispering 'make up a name'.

Our cell's floor was steeply sloped upwards. No beds, just a bare floor, and at the top was a long narrow window with bars looking out, but being dark outside. We couldn't see anything.

In the cell I began to shout - I wanted a pillow, sheet and blankets. Eventually a rough blanket was thrown in. At 6.30am a police lady with a white face opened the cell door and shouted. 'Out'.

We looked and smelled terrible; we were near Waverley Steps where there was an early cafe open. The owner felt sorry for us and gave us a cup of tea for nothing. We met a glass clearer who told us a tale about him coming from a distinguished family but was thrown out. His story was so fascinating and so interesting, but realising it was getting light, we reluctantly left, even though we wanted to know more from the glass cleaner. His story really fascinated us too.

Our YMCA was open so we crept downstairs to the bathrooms. Washed our clothes, which we put across a very large boiler. Then we crept into bed. We both slept, but was woken up by the cleaner. We told our story and she left us on our own for a while. But when we collected our clothes they were dried, but stuck together and could only be pulled apart with difficulty. Which we had to part - because these were our only clothes. They felt terribly rough.

Valerie was running out of money, we had fun walking down the high street – called Princess Street when suddenly I saw a hat shop and was mesmerized on seeing just one hat on a stand. The hat cost 10 shillings. I walked into the shop. Tried on the hat and bought it. Now I only had 6 pence. But I was so happy looking so stupid - it was a small black furry hat with two white bunny upward ears with silver studs on the ears. It didn't look well with crinkly trousers and a rough awful jumper.

Valerie thought I was bonkers. We decided to hitch a ride back home. Fortunately, a big lorry carrying furniture was driving to London. We slept on a huge bed type mattress - but was woken up by our driver 'come on - get out', which we did, reluctantly.

The driver took us into a house where there was a lady making drinks and offering doorstep cheese sandwiches, which the driver bought for both of us. Really nice of him. Then back to sleep. We eventually reached the Great North Road where we hitchhiked a lift to Wimbledon. Only three miles from my house.

After one bus ride, we were both without money? We boarded a second bus and had to tell the conductor we had no money. We filled out a form before he let us off the bus.

When we arrived home, my parents were furious - apparently my father had reported us missing to the police and Scotland Yard because I was on special medication - also he thought maybe we had been kidnapped. I was having the following week off work because my parents were going away on holiday and I had to stay behind to look after our budgie called Jimmy.

CHAPTER THREE

Jimmy

Before I travelled to Ceylon, an event at home occurred in the days when I was Jo Wright, living in Morden, Surrey. My mother used to keep budgies. She spent hours teaching them how to talk. One of them knew the address; another budgie even used to sing 'Baa, Baa, Black Sheep'. When I was fifteen, my parents decided I could be left alone while they went on holiday to the Isle of Wight. I had a big responsibility while they were away: I had to look after Jimmy, their budgie. I even took my bed downstairs to keep him company (daft me didn't think to take his cage upstairs).

On one of the rare occasions we had sunshine in England, I took great delight in having my tea in the back garden and took Jimmy with me in his cage. Thinking he should have eats too, I opened his door to give him a cream cracker. I did not know he was a strong bird. He pushed the cage fully open and flew away. Oh dear, I was devastated. I spent three days and nights knocking on neighbours' doors to look for Jimmy non-stop. On the third night, a man who was home from the merchant navy said, 'You are in luck, I have your budgie.' Then he and his sons happily handed Jimmy to me in a cage. I was over the moon. I returned their cage, and because it was so late, I let Jimmy out to have a fly and this time went to bed upstairs.

Next morning, I was in the kitchen when I suddenly heard a man with a gruff voice laughing. I was terrified and nearly jumped out of my skin. This laugh came again, and I suddenly realized Jimmy was sitting on my shoulder and laughing. I called him a few names and put Jimmy in his cage, but later on I let him fly around again. Much to my surprise, he began chatting, and I thought he was swearing and tried to listen really hard. My parents were on their way home, and I kept telling Jimmy, 'Please stop swearing. That man shouldn't have taught you to swear.' My parents were happy to be home, and then my father said, 'Come here, young lady. Where is Jimmy?' I cheekily told him he was in the lounge. 'Oh no, he isn't. That bird is not Jimmy.' Oh dear, I started crying and told him what had happened. My mum was so upset and wouldn't speak to me for days.

One afternoon, a visitor, our local vicar, arrived to talk to us about my forthcoming confirmation. My mother made a pot of tea, and we happily enjoyed tea until suddenly Jimmy landed on the tea tray and turned to our visitor and told him to (naughty word) f— off. Our visitor dropped his tea all over himself, my mother went blood red in the face, and I ran upstairs to my bedroom. Golly me, I was really in the doghouse. Jimmy stayed, and he decided to upset my parents on Sunday afternoons when they played cards with relations. He used to steal a card and show it to everyone. He was not really a very sporty bird at all, but always full of surprises.

CHAPTER FOUR

Ceylon Embassy

Then I stayed two months in the Norwegian Embassy in Cockspur Street in London and switched jobs to next door, the Ceylon Embassy, where I kept gaining promotions. Eventually, I worked for Prime Minister Donald (Dudley) Senanayake, a lovely man to work for. I first worked for him on his visit to Sir Oliver Goonetilleke, the Ceylon high commissioner. His address was 25 Grosvenor Square. Ceylon gained their independence in 1948 (India gained theirs the previous year). At the time of Mr Senanayaka's visit, I was Sir Oliver Goonetilleke's secretary. Not bad for a naughty girl with no education at all (absolutely none).

Sir Oliver had a married daughter, Sheila, who had a little daughter who was gorgeously pretty. She used to sit in front of a mirror a lot, putting on her mother's make-up. Sheila liked entertaining, and quite often, her friend Princess Margaret was invited to tea. I frequently joined them. We three used to tuck into the sandwiches and cakes brought to us. Sometimes I was too busy to join in, but altogether, I did have tea about twelve times.

CHAPTER FIVE

Hurlingham Club Age 17

After a reception in London when Princess Margaret. The King and Queen attended. Two things happened. Even though I knew - and was a friend of Princess Margaret I still had to stand in line to be presented to the King, Queen and Princess Margaret. On reaching Princess Margaret she bent forward to say something when her white bunny stole fell off her shoulders. I put out my hand to grab it when suddenly four big bodyguards appeared from nowhere - of course they retrieved her stole - but we both started to laugh.

Unfortunately, at same reception my boyfriend Ernest danced with Princess Margaret first and I was jealous and gave him up next day. I was only 17. So really, he was better off without me acting so childish.

Another event not recorded is when I was invited to Hurlingham Club Putney to witness the presentation of a gold medal to Ceylon Champion for boxing. My boss Sir Oliver Goonetileke had already left with the Prime Minister and dignitaries. Not realising the Queen was arriving to the embassy to join them. She was taking Sir Oliver's daughter Sheila and me in her car to the club.

However, when the royal car arrived there was only me to take. Sheila didn't feel well and could not join in. I explained to the Queen all had left and Shiela not well - she graciously patted car seat next to her and we four continued to the club. We had two ladies-in-waiting in the car. To our surprise we were served with a champagne dinner when joined by Princess Margaret. Three of us were served while the ladies in waiting were served sandwiches and tea. I suppose their usual fare when accompanying the Queen.

CHAPTER SIX

Princess Margaret, Shiela and Me

On one occasion, Princess Margaret had a sniffle cold. Even so, it never stopped her smoking. She had a cigarette holder which was really long, and the cigarettes were black or red with gold tips. I had asthma, so while the Princess puffed, I coughed. But one afternoon, our guest had a cough and didn't have a handkerchief. Sheila asked me to go into her bedroom to find a handkerchief, which I did. She shot me an awful look. I had picked out a lovely handkerchief with gold stitched writing and stitched flowers. Of course, Princess Margaret used it and put it in her bag. This was a special present to Sheila from the Ambassador of Brazil; Sheila treasured it. Of course, I didn't know. Needless to say, this upset Sheila, and from that day, I wasn't in her good books at all and the afternoon tea invites suddenly stopped for me. But as it happened, shortly after, I was taken to Ceylon to work with the Prime Minister of Ceylon. Our government building was on Mount Lavinia, off Colombo (now a most prestigious hotel).

My time working at the Embassy had been quite eventful and involved a lot of travel, and now I was on a ship sailing to Ceylon (now Sri Lanka). My cabin on the Arcade ship was larger than the captain's; I thought, *Poor captain*. But I was a bit cross because I wanted to swim in the pool, and I got my way eventually, only to find I was the only swimmer with four bodyguards. I just got out of the pool. I wanted to mingle with the passengers but wasn't allowed to. Silly me, I never asked why; I knew no secrets. So to this day, I still do not know the reason.

Whilst working in Ceylon I was then known as a high flyer. I worked amongst Ministers, and I am sure they had bets between themselves on who I would marry. Many kept asking me to marry them and couldn't understand it when I said no. One Minister was so cross he said, 'Why won't you marry me? I have a large plantation and racehorses. I own the biggest leather craft factory and am a minister of the government too.' I replied, 'I have to say no because I am not very old and I don't really love you.' Thinking about it now, I see how childish it was, but that was my answer to this minister. My other excuses were nearly the same. Now I wonder what love is all about!

The government office was in Mount Lavinia
Beyond was me in national daily dress (age seventeen), Colombo.

Me, on the right, sitting next to a little boy, with
Ceylon ministers, their wives, and our staff.

CHAPTER SEVEN

School Reunion

School Reunion Age nearly 18

Upon my return from Ceylon there was a Malmsbury Road School for Girls reunion. The school had been rebuilt after several parts were ruined by war damage. I was now aged seventeen and three quarters.

I cheekily went along to the reunion. Being very unpopular with all the teachers for being so naughty, I did wonder what they would say to me.

Four top girls got all the attention - known as whizz kids. One girl called Colleen was running her Mum and Dad's shop. Based in her house. She sold Sweets and cigarettes at her front door while taking in shoes for her Dad to cobble and mend.

Another girl Eileen Knight was working for Bata Shoes in Rose Hill, Carshalton. Miss Oliver was pleased saying 'Eileen, that is a nice shop - work hard and you could be shop Manager soon'..

There was a noise and in walked my friend wheeling a twin pram - she used to help me cheat at exams - which of course I never passed (not in those days!).

My friend had twins - at her age 15 became pregnant by the baker's son. The twins were beautiful. The other friend who was the brightest of all four girls, now worked for her a dad doing a paper round.

At the reunion we were expecting 500 girls, but only about 100 turned up... even so more sandwiches, cakes and drinks for the rest of us.

Many girls dwindled away and it wasn't long before I was spoken to... I just hung around waiting, when at last Miss Oliver said. 'well - Joanne - did you get that job in lines Bros; painting spots on Whakawoowoos?' (These were small tin Dalmatian white dogs with hand painted round black spots, standing on a bendable platform that when pressed, would cause the dog to fall over. I loved playing with those dogs).

I sort of looked abashed and went over to my suitcase, opened it onto a table, because I had brought home from Ceylon presents for the teachers. Little brass trays, brass ornaments, calendars of dancing girls and silk scarves. Miss Caldecott said 'where did these come from? ' I explained that I worked in Ceylon and was the Prime Minister's Secretary. Then I showed them snaps I had. Me with my Ministers and of Kandy with me in pictures with dignitaries and their children.

Miss Caldecott was so taken aback. She nastily said 'Well I'll be darned - you were the only girl to pass the Art Scholarship and now the only girl with a decent job'.

Then they really wanted to know 'how did you get that job'.

I quickly said I had joined Pitmans College with my Art Scholarship money and also signed into Pitmans in Holborn, London College and that I also worked in London during the day, too.

I told the teachers I had transferred my studies to evening classes and took day jobs to pay my way back home. I had left school at age 14 and half and did different jobs for few weeks each. I had joined a bank, then joined the Norwegian Embassy as a telephonist/typist and next door was the Ceylon Embassy, Cockspur Street, London.

When one day - during my lunch hour - I went into Ceylon Embassy to ask for the large Cricketer Poster they had in their window - (when they were throwing it away).

I was told to go back next day and instead of him giving me the poster an employee had bought me 10 cricketer pictures from a Piccadilly news stand- then invited me for lunch downstairs- where I went every day, then eventually being offered double pay to work for them. Later their Prime Minister visited. And me being me - made a tray of drinks for everyone.

I saw the Prime Minister sitting on a chair - when a front chair leg was giving way. I plonked tea tray down and rushed over and grabbed the Prime Minister - shouting Mr Sweeramani, quick, get another chair.

All was saved, but on going out the Prime Minister on seeing me 'thank you for saving my life - are you the tea girl' - I said 'no, I am Sir Oliver's Secretary ' - good he said 'can I borrow her; I have some letters to send'. Next thing I was being escorted by police cars dashing through London, sitting in a huge car with a flag on front. All very exciting - but soon squashed when the Prime Minister walked out in his pyjamas— but they were not pyjamas - it was his home Traditional leisure wear.

(Digressing a bit. the Prime Minister lived in No. 2, Park Road. London. Just a front door - no windows either side —- but inside was awesome- like a big park with apartments surrounding all overlooking grass verges, flower beds and a middle lake with a high fountain. All was beautiful.)

After this visit/taking dictation/going back to Embassy to type, it was decided I should work in Ceylon.   This is because our two embassies were closing- only 21 Addison Crescent was in full swing where I was trying to do stock taking - a daunting job.

So, I told the teachers briefly as much as I could – 'Well' - said Miss Caldecott, 'I am giving up teaching, It's all a farce the amount of time segregating bright students to help them even more'.

Anyway, all was forgiven because they were surprised that I was the only one who had a good job. The teachers loved their presents, with promises that they would keep in touch - but never have.

CHAPTER EIGHT

Hole in Heart

I left Ceylon and went back to Morden in Surrey, but I wasn't home long before I became very ill with heart trouble and spent a long time in the Royal London Hospital, Whitechapel. Two years went by before an English surgeon of eminence, Mr Vernon Thomson, flew his equipment over from the USA to set up in the Hospital to operate on me and six others. A Dutch lady in the USA had been operated on but caught the flu two months later at home in Maryland; her mother never thought to send for a doctor, and unfortunately, the Dutch lady died. Mr Vernon Thompson operated on seven of us but, unfortunately for him, my six companions died, leaving me the sole survivor. After that, the operation changed. I was told that later patients were made to be cold before their operation. I hate the cold, so I was glad it wasn't me. This was the first hole-in-a-heart operation to be successful worldwide. There was a lady who had a heart operation in 1948, but it was not a hole in the heart; it was an investigatory operation.

The press were very keen to get my story for many years, particularly the *Evening Standard* and the *Star*. Sylvia Cheeseman, the Olympic Games runner, was my reporter for a long time, and David Bailey was my photographer. Seven years later, when he attended and photographed my wedding to Ron Taylor (my holiday scrumping friend), David Bailey still worked for the *Star*, as well as for himself. Even three years after that, he photographed me in hospital during the birth of my first daughter, Karen Jane. All in all, the reporting in London lasted for over twenty years (then I went to live in the north of England)!

CHAPTER NINE

Billy Graham

An evangelist was preaching in White City. I belonged to his choir of 100, and our choir master was called Chris. One evening, while singing, I suddenly had the feeling that someone was pulling me. I rose from my seat, passed my colleagues, and walked down a few steps in front of 35,000 people. I walked to the front of Billy Graham, the evangelist. Mr Graham called to the audience to join me. Hundreds of people came, and together we went into a side room, where councillors talked to us. I had a wonderful feeling; I wanted to shout praises from the rooftops.

Travelling back to Morden on the underground train, the train was full of passengers who were all singing the hymn 'This Is My Story' together. A few months later, I was baptised in my local church as a born-again Christian. Eventually I became a Seventh-Day Adventist, which is where I worship today. We attend church on Saturdays, because the fourth commandment states, 'Keep the Sabbath holy.' Of course, the Sabbath is a Saturday in any language.

Later on, I was baptised again in a river in America at the same time as my granddaughters Sarah and Suzannah (Sandralee's daughters). This occasion was so beautiful. The congregation stood on a bridge overlooking the lake; they threw white flowers into the water, and hymns were played. It was a very joyous and memorable occasion.

CHAPTER TEN

After London Hospital

I felt a bit better after returning from a convalescence of three months in St Anna's in Lucerne, Switzerland. I had learned a lot by restudying. I walked into a job bureau in London. They asked me for my curriculum vitae, and on seeing my previous jobs, they sent me away, put me on their payroll, and said they would get in touch when a job vacancy for me occurred.

Two months later, they sent for me. They had a job for me, and I was to attend an interview to see Mr Ernest Marples. Afterwards, I was working for MP Ernest Marples, postmaster general (later on, he became minister of transport). Mr Marples owned Marples Ridgeway, and he lived in his offices at No. 2 Lygon Place, Victoria (near Westminster). I was his PA secretary, doing work for Ridgeway and in Westminster. The Ridgeway firm was building the M1 motorway with Cubitts, Holland & Hanson, and it has turned out to be a fine motorway. This job lasted awhile, until I left to go into modelling. I enjoyed modelling in adverts and appearing on large posters which drooped behind the

Joanne with Duchess Potato chipper/peeler. =Backdrop - behind London Underground trains.

London Underground trains. Once, while standing in Leicester Square Underground, I saw that there were three posters.

One was of me posing behind a duchess potato peeler; another was of me holding up a tin of Maynard toffees, wearing a big bonnet and saying 'ooooooh'; and the third was of my hand holding a musical lighter. This job was very varied and interesting. Different well-known people came into the studio, like Arthur Askey (he visited three times when we were advertising Pye television, and he brought Sabrina with him). Jack Train came in, and I bored him by telling him all about the film called *Quatermass*. He had a straight face and was so polite. Otherwise, he was a hilarious comedian. We were waiting for my boss, who was late.

Even so, I decided to leave and join a company called Bowaters, the paper magnam firm in Knightsbridge. After six promotions, I began working for Sir Vansitart Bowater, the owner. This was an interesting job. Sir Eric built a cinema in the basement, which was great fun to go to when a good film was on offer. In those days, this cinema cost £35,000.

Later on, I was called back to London Hospital for photographs. Suddenly I saw men with yellow hats scurrying by. My photographic staff was gone. I was so engrossed in watching this machine above me when firemen came dashing in and wheeled me along the corridor. Unbeknown to me, next door had been blown up. A Pathé newsreel van followed me. I was laughing my head off at them and waving, though I had no idea they were Pathé News until I saw myself on a cinema screen.

CHAPTER ELEVEN

Nightclub

When I was in my early twenties I met two film stars. One died while he was young, but his film star ex-wife is still alive. The other lad film star is still married to his second wife. It is difficult to relate this when true names cannot be mentioned, but one night my film star friends drove me home. One wanted to come into my house, but it was two in the morning and my dad woke up. He was cross at being woken up; he opened the bedroom window and threw a bucket of water over him. I said, 'Dad, you shouldn't have done that. He is a film star.' But because my friend was all wet, they both spent the night in a Turkish bath (open all night at a cost of fourteen shillings). The reason I relate this is that a tragedy occurred. The young film star wife of my other friend believed her husband was having an affair, which he was not, and that night, she gassed herself. It was the most terrible happening, and shortly after, my friend died of cancer. I went to court for the suicide hearing, only to know that the answer for the young girl was that she couldn't perfect the Queen's English. I had already given my statement in a rear office, explaining about her husband not going straight home that night. So the reason the coroner gave was not true. At the time, my friend was separated from his film star wife. Needless to say, I never saw either of them again.

Shortly after, I decided to go for a Turkish bath myself after night school and, because I was a daredevil, decided to call in to the Salisbury Pub for lemonade afterwards. I was invited by a lone drinker drinking a very nice red wine, and I accepted one glass. Even the barman joined us. The drinker was Rex Harrison; he was in the middle of filming (he did *Doctor Dolittle*). He was staying in Bloomsbury Avenue, London. Obviously he felt he wanted to chill out in his local. I did not mention films; we talked about travelling, and he asked me what my ambitions were. I said, 'Just to be happy.' How lame was that—to have no other ambition?

One interesting episode for me was my time spent in Alexandra Palace in 1949, making a TV film. The show was *This Is Martarabotom Voice of the East*. It was my role to begin the programme by beating a tom-tom (bongos). My nails were painted black, and I wore an orange sari full of jewels. On the programme were two dancers, Margaret and John; they danced a scene from *Swan Lake*. The stage was held up by six men on their knees under the stage.

The next dancer was Margarite, from Spain, brandishing castanets and giving a most beautiful heel-clicking Spanish dance. There was a group of Chinese men sitting on the floor, playing music by banging different glasses with small steel rods; these glasses were filled with water. It was so musical. Lastly, there was an Indian girl dancing in the traditional classic Indian style. I ended the show beating the bongos again. I was well paid for my effort. We broke off for the news when it was introduced by McDonald Hobley.

Around the studio, there were little black-and-white small-screen TVs. This studio was in a lower basement at the end of a series of corridors; it was eerie. I said to McDonald, 'I am not very happy at these small screens all in black and white when everybody here is so colourful. I am never buying a television until it is in colour.' In all seriousness, he said to me, 'There will never be colour TV. In fact, there won't be men on the moon either.' Looking back now, I see how wrong he was! And yes, my first TV was a coloured one. As a rule, the general public did not have a TV (unless they were rich), but most embassies had one.

CHAPTER TWELVE

Bowaters (1955–1963)

Sir Eric Vansitart Bowater, the owner of Bowaters, had a head office based in Knightsbridge, London (where I worked). It was a very fine building with 800 employees. The Bowater organisation was responsible for papermaking. There were two outlet factories, one in Gravesend and the other in Northfleet. In the beginning, tree-fell men cut trees down in Newfoundland; they stripped the branches off, then rolled the trees downhill to the water's edge. Bowaters had fourteen ships headed by dry-land captain Dumar. My ex-husband, Ron Taylor, was the steamship accountant. It was because he worked there that I changed my job to work in Bowaters; I could see it was a fine establishment to work in, and I also kept an eye on him in case he was chasing the secretaries. Whichever is true, I now cannot remember!

The workmen at the water's edge in Newfoundland used to load the trees on to the cargo ships. These ships would sail to either factory in England. The logs were put through the largest of large scraping machines. After a few processing techniques, the results would be cardboard, Bowater Scottissue (toilet paper sheets), boxes for the Scottissue, and Bowater Eburite cardboard, which were made into boxes under that style name. The boxes were all sizes. There was another paper company, named Reed, but it was not as large as Bowaters at the time. The machines also produced newsprint paper, huge rolls of which were sent to Fleet Street (which was famous for newspaper outlets) for the *Daily Telegraph*, the *Observer*, the *Financial Times*, the *Star*, the *Evening Standard*, the *Daily Worker*, *People*, and many more. Also, thicker and even shinier paper was produced to be made into magazines.

At one stage, I was secretary to the director, Mr Young Scottissue, but he returned to the Bowater Birmingham office, which left me as a spare part. When Bowaters bought a company called Hunts, retaining its owner, Mr Gordon W. Ingle, I was quickly transferred to set up new offices for him and me. He then became Sir Eric's right-hand man as group accountant. My work involved producing huge spreadsheets once a month; no computers were around then to help in these equations.

On the first day of his appointment, Mr Ingle attended my lunchtime prayer meeting. I had founded a Christian society for thirty of the staff. Every Tuesday at lunchtime, I engaged outside speakers to join us for a very light lunch and a peaceful time together for a short while. It was good news for both Mr Ingle and me to be together in the Christian group on his first day. It somehow brought us close together, and he never wanted me to be replaced. At that time, I was only on loan, but he managed to cement my appointment until Sir Eric's secretary left. Then I was transferred to work for Sir Eric as well. But Mr Ingle insisted I was shared. In March 1961, I had to leave Bowaters because I was expecting Karen Jane, my first daughter, who arrived in the world on 1 May 1961.

Bowaters had a very fine reception desk manager, a retired army major, Ronald Brittain, MBE. He had the loudest voice in the British Army. Outside people often came to reception just to meet him. He was one of the kindest men I ever had the pleasure to meet. One night, it was very funny. My adopted cousin Horace, who was on leave from the army, came to meet me and entered the building (which, incidentally, was one of the most beautiful buildings in London; all the Italian marble was imported by Sir Eric when it was being built). On this particular evening, my cousin began walking up the beautiful ornate stairs when Ronald Brittain shouted 'Pick 'em up, lad!' at the top of his voice. My cousin fell all the way down the stairs. He must have learned to fall, because he didn't hurt himself. Office people heard this, so there was a rush to pick Horace up.

Ronald was such a character. When we had large receptions in the social room, Ronald would parade around in his uniform, pretending he was putting everything in order. In a loud, bold voice, he would announce the guests as they walked in. Sir Eric loved the razzmatazz which surrounded his famous reception employee, who had the largest-sounding voice.

One evening, we invited world championship table tennis winners to give an exhibition in-house against me and my partner because we were Bowater champions. Also, two Bowater lads were double winners. This girl and I challenged the Chinese Rowe twins, Empire Games medal winners. Our two lads played side by side against the one-man games winner (I have forgotten his name). The evening was in full swing when Sir Eric announced his surprise as this girl and I and the Rowe twins walked in dressed in whites, the standard dress for exhibition tennis players (with very short skirts too). Our game ended in hysterics. My partner walked out, leaving me to run around the table after the Rowe twins. Their ball would bounce on my side of the table but would somehow turn itself round to go back to them. I tried but failed to hit the ball many times. Everyone was laughing at my antics when I was trying to hit the ball. In the end, two men came in with a stretcher and laid me on it, put a glass of bubbly in my hand and big flowers on top of me, and carried me out. This was all crazy while being very funny.

Our two lads didn't do much better. One lad walked away, while the other one tried to take the game seriously but got nowhere. He unfortunately got very cross because he wasn't showing his own skill as our champion tennis player. His world-famous opponent would not allow him to hit the ball properly. It was an exhibition, but obviously our lad lost miserably; he wasn't happy about it. Meanwhile, I had a nice drink, a ride out, a bunch of flowers to take home, and a memory of the event, which was hilarious.

Sir Eric had a cinema built in the basement, and the only way guests could reach the cinema was to take the lift to the twelfth floor (where my office was). The guests would gingerly walk into my office to the discrete small lift which went straight to Sir Eric's office, where they would be greeted and refreshed and would then take his lift straight down to the private £35,000 cinema. There was no other way to reach the cinema; it was only open to invitation only. Because I cannot name names, as you can imagine, very many famous people were guests of Sir Eric in his cinema, including a male member of the royal family. Captain Duma would often be amongst the guests. He was Scottish and loved his whisky (of course, this is tell tailing). He fell down more than once in my lift after a drink, with the doors opening, closing, opening, and closing, until I pulled him out. But I shouldn't really tell tales. He was such a jolly character; I loved him.

Unfortunately, for some reason, this beautiful building is now no more. I took a friend from the USA (who I had met on a plane) to London for a few days. I met this lady on a half-hour flight from Philadelphia to Erie. She had wanted to go to England. I said, 'Come over, stay with me,' and gave her my address, so she did. Hazel came and stayed for three weeks. Anyway, when I went to show Hazel the Bowater House in Knightsbridge, it wasn't there. I was horrified. Even to this day, I can't think of any reason such a beautiful building should be pulled down.

The personal officers in Bowaters were a man and a lady. I have unfortunately forgotten the man's name. They were attached to the three As (Amateur Athletic Association), and both went to Japan to arrange for the Olympic Games. Miss Maria Hartman was the female personnel manager. Although she was a secretary to the Amateur Athletic Association, she loved her job in Bowaters, so she tried not to let her appointment in the AAA take her away from the office too often.

After I left, two years passed, and Maria Hartman telephoned me to ask if I could possibly come to work in Bowaters for two weeks. Even though I was expecting my second baby, I said yes and took Karen to stay with her grandma in London. My task was very sad. I stayed with Maria Hartman, who had a flat in Park Lane overlooking Hyde Park. Every day I would go to work and be locked in a room alone, except for a postman who came twice a day and anyone I invited, because Olympic runner Lillian Board had died of cancer. She had gone to a clinic in Austria to get well and be saved. A lot of letters with money in them were being sent to Maria with specific instructions. One cheque was to be divided this way: one amount to parents, one amount to AAA, and one amount to Lillian's fiancé. Sometimes the cash was just for one person or an amount of cash would be split two ways. But there were loads of these letters. There was no computer, so I opened three large books; everything in each letter had to be recorded in detail, including cross cheques. Also, there was another address book with the names, addresses, and telephone numbers of the senders. I wrote thank-you letters to each and every one of them. Every day, the manager of the Barclays Bank near Harrods would arrive, and I would give him the money and show him the accounts so far, which he ticked as read. It was a sad time to be involved in Lillian's tragedy, but Maria Hartman wouldn't transfer anyone from the office staff to do this work. Her excuse was 'Joanne, you are the only person I can trust'. I have always rated this as the best compliment I have ever had.

Also, she said, 'I still remember the kind heart you have. You used to feed the tramp in Hyde Park every lunchtime.' I never knew I was being watched. The tramp was called George. It's true, every lunchtime I did give him a sandwich, but I used to go skiff rowing every weekday (even in the winter). My skiff had one seat which moved up and down while I was rowing. But about George, I found him a job and got him clothes from my then-fiancé's father (they were the same size). The job was to deliver letters to firms in London. Taking George and the letters either by bus or taxi if urgent. Trouble was, when George arrived at the firms, they would give him cake and a cup of tea, and later on, his employer said, 'I am sorry, I will have to lay George off. He takes too long to deliver letters.' I think George then found himself a job clearing up cups in a tea/coffee cafe.

I invited George to my wedding too. Mr Taylor Snr gave clothes for George to wear. George did turn up; I never told anyone he was a tramp. Anyway, while I was sitting at the top table, I noticed he was attempting to take his jacket off, and to my shock and horror, round his waist he had frayed string holding his trousers up, tied in a big bow. I shouted, 'George, put your coat back on!' Eighty guests turned round to look at him. I think I must have turned blood red because I had embarrassed myself. A lot of my guests then saw he was a tramp, even though I had combed his hair.

Such is life. Everyone acts crazy at times, and I am no exception. But goodness knows what happened to George, because after our wedding, I went to live in Essex and couldn't find George in Hyde Park any more. No one knew where he was, so I had to stop looking. After losing Lillian Board, I lost touch with Maria Hartman and friends in Bowaters.

During the time I was expecting my second daughter, I was very ill, and my doctor wanted me to be completely looked after. There wasn't anyone he could think of besides my relations in America. My parents could look after my little daughter, Karen Jane, but not me as well. So in October 1962, I flew from Heathrow to New York to stay with my many relations there.

The plane journey was interesting because I travelled with racing driver John Surtees, his wife, his director, and his mechanic, who let me sit by the window. Even though I was pregnant, they wanted me to travel with them to Mexico, where John was racing. Of course, I could not do that. Then on leaving the plane, I was asked to stay seated. We were travelling economy, but when everyone had left the plane, we all left by the first-class exit because the press were waiting for John and his party to arrive. I was asked to wave, which I did. Then at my relations' place, we watched TV, and there I was, coming down the plane steps, waving at everyone. What a laugh.

While on this visit, I was so well-looked-after; my doctor was right. My uncle and aunt treated me to the pictures at Radio City. Apart from when the Rockets danced onstage, there was an extra supporting feature. I saw that on each side of the stage, there were television screens. Suddenly there was an announcement: 'Ladies and gentleman, you are about to see the first colour pictures. See our two TV screens, which are coming directly from Japan via Telstar.' Suddenly the TVs were lit up by a military band from Barbados. They were all dressed in gold with red trims, playing wonderful music. It was spectacular. Then the curtains opened, and this band was performing on our stage.

This then was a new beginning for colour TV, which did not reach England until 1968. And yes, it was then that I had my own colour TV, which McDonald Hobley had said would never happen. He was wrong about men going to the moon too.

MRS. JOAN TAYLOR attended at Wickford Congregational Church for the christening of her second daughter. In 1955 Mrs. Taylor was the first patient to have a successful hole-in-the-heart operation.

CHAPTER THIRTEEN

Leaving the Marriage

Quite often during our time battling with the elements and everyday life, there is a hitch which is uncharacteristic. This happened to me in 1968. Realising, of course, that this is backtracking. I went through a period of unhappiness nearing depression. My marriage was failing, and I left home eventually, taking my two daughters with me. We three moved into a house in St Anne's, Lancashire. The rent was thirty pounds a month. This amount was made of four rentals and me and my daughters on the ground floor. I had a job in the civil service, and the girls, ages five and a half and four, attended school.

I became ill and was taken to Blackpool Victoria Hospital, where they transferred me to a ward, a very quiet ward. My parents (from down south) turned up with my then-husband. I was shouted at because my eldest daughter's hair wasn't short enough. I felt very alone because I had no friends. The ward sister told my mother, father, and husband to leave and not come back. Later I was wheeled into a very crowded surgical ward. My bed was put in the middle of the ward, with a light bulb over it, and I was told not to move for ten days. I was obviously still more than depressed, especially at being told off because Karen's hair hadn't been cut for a while (she had such lovely golden curls; it was nice just to see them). It wasn't long before I actually left the marital home which I had personally furnished.

I gained work in a supermarket, and the manager gave me a loan (out of my wages) to clothe my daughters and myself. I had left with only nightclothes on and no shoes, only slippers, taking no money. At 9 p.m., in the rain, a family found us in my old car (a green Morris Minor) and took us into their home. They took the girls to school in boys' clothes, and I was found a job in the supermarket across. There was a bit of a difference, as my last job in London was as PA secretary to Sir Eric Vansitart Bowater (the paper magnate in Knightsbridge) six years previous. However, I settled down and even met a boy who later became my husband, named Graham. He and his grandmother loved my little girls.

Graham and I eventually became engaged and rented a house together, which I sublet. He and others rented flatlets, and the girls and I occupied the ground floor. The girls both continued in their schools; I still worked in Premium Bonds, whereas Graham worked for Tesco. One Saturday afternoon, my landlady and her husband visited for the rents. I didn't have anyone else's money from anywhere. A tenant named Linda had gone to Leeds for a long weekend. Graham had already boarded a train to go to Scotland. A top-flat couple had had a row and had absconded without leaving me their money, and a couple in another flat had gone for a week's holiday, leaving no rent. My £6 was not enough for my visitors.

All my excuses fell on deaf ears, and they evicted me. They put all my house clothes and personal clothes—everything—out on the street. They filled two suitcases with toys and a few of the girls' things and put them in the basement; these were found by someone after a few months and returned to me. Then the landlady said, 'You can go upstairs into the attic flat,' and just handed me my coat and my handbag. I remember walking upstairs, looking at the shower room and seeing a broken shower, and walking into the lounge and sitting on the floor. That was Saturday, just after 3 p.m. Linda arrived back on Tuesday and decided I was ill. She called Dr Bilbey, who confirmed I was ill since I could not remember anything. My two daughters were already with their grandmothers down south for their school holidays, so no one was there to talk to Dr Bilbey when he decided I should be in hospital for my own safety (he explained this to me much later on). He arranged for transport to take me to a hospital.

A girl in a red car took me to Lancaster Moor Hospital, where I was immediately taken to my own small bedroom, which had a double door, a huge black potty on the floor, and no light bulbs (the lights were behind a casing in the ceiling). The bed had sewn-around sheets and no pillow. I was asked every day, 'What is your name, and what day is it?' I got really cross. I kept telling them every day, 'You know what my name is, and it's Saturday. Don't keep asking me.' Then one day, I got so fed up I leaned forward and butted the doctor in the nose. Needless to say, I got into so much trouble over this; I was transferred to a room across which had no locked door. There was a proper bed and pillow and duvet; it had a chair and a wardrobe, but still no mirror. Also, there was a bathroom for me next door, with a washbasin, so I could at last wash myself.

Of course, I did not know my name or what I looked like or that I was a mother and used to be married or anything else. I couldn't even speak properly. I would join the dining room. One lady would walk around on her heels all day. Another lady would be sitting and counting her fingers up to ten and beginning again. I would be sitting in the corner of a settee, crying all the time. Also, there was a little lady who kept wanting to give me 'rubber lip' kisses. Ugh. It was horrible. Then one day she crashed a plant pot over my head. There was earth and mud everywhere, and it hurt. A huge bump took over my head. I remember being floored quite often by a lady who thought I had cigarettes, which, of course, I didn't have any of.

I then saw myself on the back of a big spoon. I thought the image was upside down, and my face was sideways both sides and fat. I had a horrible face. After that, I never ever wanted to look in a mirror at my horrible face. I had my hair cut with a pudding basin over my head; the nurse would cut round it. I suppose I looked like a monk. I was administered shock treatment, which was a terrible experience. I thought my eyes were popping out of my head and would never go back, and the sickness was terrible. After some treatments, the powers that be stopped this practice. The machines were taken away.

Occasionally, between crying, I had flashes of seeing small children and hearing names being said to me in my head and seeing outside images, like a bus and a park and two dogs. These images sometimes wouldn't go away. Also, I was sent to help in the big laundry room full of machines, so of course, I met other people. This daily routine lasted three months.

There was a phone call from my boyfriend, who was in Scotland and had been looking for me for two months. Eventually, my doctor told him to try Lancaster Moore. At the time of Graham's first call, the ward sister said, 'Mrs Taylor, we have a telephone call for you.' I wouldn't go. I said, 'I am not Mrs Taylor.' The sister phoned Graham back, and his voice sparked a memory slot. I actually said, 'How are you, Graham?' That surprised the staff. He phoned again a few more times. He told the sister his surname and said it was my surname too, because before becoming ill, I had changed my name to Kendall via a deed poll. This must have been why I didn't recognise the name Taylor.

I was told in hospital in the first week that I was three months pregnant, which should have stopped them from giving me all sorts of pills or the shock treatments. The nurses invited me to play cards, which I did; beforehand, I played bridge a lot. They noticed I was improving in health. I was taken into Lancaster by bus with a male doctor and a nurse, and we had lunch out too. We did a bit of shopping. A few days later, the doctor took me to Glasgow on a train, and Graham met us and took me back to where he was living. I then met Graham's work people, and they explained that they were sorry he couldn't complete the course, mainly because of all the time he spent trying to find me. They were pleased to see I was better, since they knew that I had suffered a breakdown coupled with amnesia, which they said 'must have been awful for you'.

I left Glasgow and went to St Anne's, where my ex-husband met me, saying Dr Bilbey and a policeman had visited him to get permission to see if I could stay with him and my daughters until my fiancé and his mother found a flat for us near her in Blackpool. He said yes. Then my girls gave me big hugs; they were the two little girl images I kept seeing in my head. I was still recovering from being so ill.

I was told to go up to the front bedroom. It was dark outside, so I did. But at 9 p.m., I called out. An old man called George came to see me. 'What's wrong?' I told him I had stomach pains and asked if he could call Dr Bilbey. He brought me a glass of water and said, 'It's only wind.' However, I then shouted, 'Quick, come in here!' My youngest, age three and a half, came in (she began private school at three because she missed her sister while going to primary school). Little Sandralee was all bleary-eyed. 'What is the matter, Mummy?' I said to go to the phone in the hallway, ring 999, call an ambulance, say Mummy is not well, and say the address, which she knew. So she did. She phoned, saying, 'Quick, my mummy's dying,' and gave the address. She ran upstairs and got into her bed.

Quickly, there was a bang on the door; a medic had arrived. He came upstairs and found me and said to my ex-husband, 'Your wife is in labour.' He said, 'We thought she had wind.' The medic ran out, saying he was going to send an ambulance. Unfortunately, as soon as the medic left, the baby began coming out. I shouted out. My ex-husband came and saw what was happening. He wrapped the newly born baby boy in my nightie and took everything away. The ambulance took me to a hospital; the late-night surgeon couldn't understand where the baby was, and I was too out of it to say much.

Two weeks later, I left the hospital when my boyfriend and his lovely mum took me to a flat she had found for us, next door to her. When we both had to begin working again, for my part, it took a while to get adjusted, but eventually all fell into place.

CHAPTER FOURTEEN

Time Marches on from 1968

Living in Blackpool after my ordeal in Lancaster Moor, it was time for me to continue with my job in the civil service. The whole time I was ill in Lancaster Moor, I was still in the employment of the civil service Ernie in Lytham, St Anne's. Eventually I married my fiancé, Graham, and we bought a little house. We went into the entertainment business. Graham used to write songs and play the keyboard, and he was in a new band of four

named Unity Jones. We four had a very happy household. Graham used to entertain the girls by singing his own songs. This was an exciting time for me; it involved travelling around on weekends and going to gigs. Also, we produced the government newsletter. Graham would write it, and I would type and edit it. Also, he was the producer and I was the administrator for a play group called Pre-Bond Players. We took our plays to a local theatre, and once a month, we took two large coaches to Manchester Free Trade Hall to see groups such as Free; Yes; Pink Floyd; The Who; Mark Bolyn; Emerson, Lake, and Palmer; and many other well-known groups. Once we went to a big local shed (now a fine brick theatre known as Lytham Theatre); it had no seats, and we sat on the floor. There was an untidy group with very untidy long hair, and their noise was unbelievably awful—at least, that was what I thought. It turned out we were watching the very first performance of Genesis. My comments afterwards—'That group won't get anywhere'—fell on deaf ears.

It was my fault that Graham became a musician. When I met him, he wasn't musical, except on his grandmother's piano; he used to bang on it, and I thought I could detect a future talent creeping in if given the chance. He did have many apple drums covered in masses of Sellotape; he used to bang on these, making a not-so-terrible noise. He eventually became a professional drummer, then a guitarist, and then a keyboard player on a Hammond organ. To this day, he still plays musical instruments elsewhere!

We did marry, and altogether, our time together was enjoyable and lasted eight years.

But due to circumstances beyond my control, we parted and went our separate ways.

CHAPTER FIFTEEN

Ada, My Pets, and Cilla

My mother and me with Ada.

There was a time I had a friend named Ada Kay. She is a writer; one title of hers, *Falcon*, must still be in libraries. Ada was reincarnated from King James IV. An account of her reincarnation is on the Internet at present, especially Google. I went to her wedding when she married Mr Stewart (I was her bridesmaid). She used to spend weekends at my parents' house; every Saturday, my mother would make her a very large Cornish pasty, and then she would fall asleep for several hours. My mother thought she never ate much during the week. She wrote a play called *The Last Man from Sparton*, which won her a BBC contract. The play was on the radio and on TV, and she wrote the last few episodes of *The Grove Family*, a television series which the Queen Mother liked.

Ada went to live in Edinburgh and spent a lot of time in research to fill in history. There was a very large wall painting in the national gallery of a royal court household, and she told the gallery restorer, 'If you remove the dog from the painting, you will find me at the age of four underneath.' This was true. The dog was painted out, and yes, King James, as a boy, was underneath.

She often spent her time in Longleat. But I fear Ada may not be with us any more, because about six years ago, I was disturbed and thought about her, mostly at night. Just as suddenly, the disturbances stopped.

* * *

Going back in time, I had many pets, all at different times: two rabbits, two boxer dogs, a

Labrador, two cats, and a budgie called Beauty, who could talk. Also, when I was living in Wickford, Essex, in 1960, there was Bimbo, a Shetland pony who had the freedom of the avenue. There was no danger; there was only a field at the bottom. One Sunday morning, I was peeling potatoes when Bimbo poked his head through the open window and took the potato from me. He used to amuse the children around with his antics. He was a lovable little character.

* * *

Cilla and me.

When I was working in the civil service, I met Cilla Black, her husband Bobby, and their doggy called Sofie. On my first encounter with Sofie, she floored me. She was a tall raggy grey dog, and she had jumped at me and proceeded to lick my face. Cilla had to take me upstairs and reapply my make-up. This was because she had agreed to cut the ribbon for our Civil Service Fete Day, which was always a grand event when Graham and I were officiating. I took Sofie for a walk on many occasions. When Cilla moved to London, I went to stay a few times. It was an awful loss when poor Cilla was taken, just as Bobby, her husband, was previously.

CHAPTER SIXTEEN

1974–1981

By this time, I had changed jobs and was working for British Aerospace in Warton and then later in Weybridge, Surrey, when I had to live with my parents because my father was ill, having had leg amputations, and my mother had a nervous breakdown.

My job was as secretary to Mr Les Dennis, the general manager. We had 8,000 employees to look after. Also, we had to cope with the IRA infiltration of bombs. I had a phone call, and I became suspicious. The caller was broad Irish, and I believed the message. Yes, there were six bombs inside. All 8,000 employees were outside the factory while these bombs were being found. This bomb alert often happened after that first incident.

My boss, Mr Dennis, and I decided to drive to Woking, and we had lunch with his friend, Mr Freddie Laker. I was invited later for dinner with Mr Laker; he worked so hard trying to keep his Skytrain, but other airlines were all against him. Mr Laker had a beautiful estate in Epsom, with so many racehorses—the other love of his life. His spread wasn't too far from where my parents lived. Freddie (called Lal) visited my parents, taking his big white Rolls-Royce, which took the cul-de-sac space outside; this amused my mum and dad. He was a busy man and sometimes worked eighteen hours a day.

My time in Surrey was spasmodic, because some weekends, I had to drive 350 miles each way to return to St Anne's to join my two daughters. This lasted for thirteen months until I eventually left British Aerospace because the travelling proved too difficult to continue. My father died, and my mother moved to stay with me in St Anne's. This move out of British Aerospace took me into the racehorse business—twelve, to be precise.

I joined a Mr Lee and his complex; he had a farm, 600 battery hens on-site, 12 racehorses, and meal-making turrets. We employed farm staff for help with the chickens (Mr Lee hoped his son would help, but he was a good tennis player and preferred the court life instead). Also, we had two grooms for the horses.

This was an exciting experience until I decided to go to college, then university. I also did Open

University. The course name was Making Sense of Society. This was a brilliant course. Also, I had to later on get a Chamber of Commerce teachers training certificate.

After leaving study, a more eventful life began to take place. Not yet finished with my studies, I began working in the six-week break by opening three businesses: Kenlan Finance Brokers, JLK Business Services, and JLK Quick Services.

All the businesses took off when I joined in with JLK Quick Services by hiring a very large lorry named Kirk from Lancaster; it had a hopper unit and uniform for sandblasting. So I went into the sandblasting business in Great Harwood and unfortunately put my friend David in the business as general manager. David found the jobs in sandblasting as well as farm renovations. So I hired eight university colleagues and two friends to carry out this work. I carried on with studies, but Open University gave me later time to carry out these businesses while still finding twenty-one hours of study time. But things went wrong.

CHAPTER SEVENTEEN

Love Awry

Way back in 1981, everything was rosy in my life, which turned out to be a misapprehension. I was a college student, and during the holidays, I worked my own businesses, doing sandblasting and farmhouse renovations with the help of eight workers. I hired a van with all the sandblast equipment included, hired a compressor, and bought silver sand. The workers were all my colleagues from college. Also, I had a friend, David, who was my manager and who was very good at getting jobs for us.

David was suave and a chauvinist, and I, being gullible, fell for his charm, having known him for several months. When he decided to ask me to marry him, silly me said yes. At the time, I had two new cars on hire purchase, one for me and one for David to use in the businesses. I had a team of workers for sandblasting and for renovating a farm.

Unfortunately the marriage liaison after two days was over-coupled with the loss of my three businesses, two cars and house contents. I was granted an annulment.

I had to pay my business creditors as well. They all sympathised with me, but it took me over twelve years to pay for everything I owed. I worked so hard seven days a week. During this time too, my house had subsidence, and I was forced to move, which unfortunately happened even though there was a housing boom going on in England. I am still living in the second house.

My life now is very good, with me having got over this drastic experience, and it has left me with this thought: *Be careful from now on*. Now I am able to detect who is a con man and who isn't. Before, I wore rose-coloured glasses, but I have also learned to say no.

CHAPTER EIGHTEEN

Life After Studies

For a brief time following the collapse of my three businesses and closure of my studies, I joined a local (Head Office) company named 'Small Businesses' as an Executive.

The members, for a small annual fee, had access to Small Businesses should their own business meet trouble.

One evening a deputation of five - 2 from Head Office, 1 from Essex, 1 from Middlesex, and 1 from Kent. We met in London to attend a pre-arranged appointment with Sir Robert Sheldon. Treasury Minister in Westminster Government Offices.

We each had a case to relate of unfairness to the five businesses. My case related to an Army Camp store near camp gates, opened especially or soldiers to buy daily items needed.

Unfortunately the owner had overlooked to pay his tax on time, when one morning, before the store opened, Tax Officials broke into the store and took out perishable goods. Upon opening the store the Manager's wife broke down - she had to be taken to hospital. The Manager had to cease the employment of 15 staff. The store was shut, after which the Manager spent all his time in hospital visiting his wife.

Eventually, he contacted our office when I took his case to investigate. My explanation with the Minister resulted in the Manager being awarded £3,000 with a promise that this situation will be attended to.

Next day, the National newspapers held multiple stories about the Tax Officials' behaviour. It ordered that never again will Tax Officials break into or enter any premises in the absence of the business Owner and not before 9am.

I always think this is quite an achievement, which I am proud of. The other business mishaps were then researched by the Treasury, and in every case, there was a satisfactory outcome.

CHAPTER NINETEEN

Travelling in India (1984)

During my time in India, I actually made some awesome journeys. Apart from later going to Goa for a two-week holiday, I also took some great train journeys. My friend of many years, Captain Kiran K., who was born in Thane in Bombay, India, had business in Calcutta. He invited his wife, Geraldine, and me to meet him in Calcutta for three weeks, then go on to New Delhi for two weeks, and a further invitation to visit the Taj Mahal in Agra. It was one of my wishes to see the Taj Mahal, so I was very excited at the whole idea.

Geraldine and I set off to catch a train from Bombay to Calcutta; the journey was thirty-five hours. This entailed three meals a day and a most comfortable bed each. Making the bed was the easiest of processes. In tourist class, each seat had three people, and also, a side seat could seat three. Then there was a corridor stretching the whole length of the long train. A seat was in the middle of one side. When we wanted to stretch out, whether day or night, we three stood up, and at the flick of a switch, the seat/bed would rise and click into place. A thick seat underneath would come up, and a back panel would come forward. The whole process only took a few seconds. The seats were made of thick brown genuine leather.

On boarding the train, we were each given a packet (it contained a new sheet, new blanket, and new pillow). Our luggage was taken from us, labelled, and stored in a special luggage carriage. We could keep our small bag of nightclothes and personal belongings. Each carriage had a bathroom for washing and a changing room. The fare for the journey was, I think, just £8. There was also a third bed above my middle bed. The third person had to climb up a ladder to use this bed. In normal trains, this section is usually the luggage rack.

The whole journey was spectacular. Along the top end of my bed was a window which opened, so throughout the journey, I took some awesome photographs. India scenery is forever changing outlooks along the train journeys.

Our time in Calcutta was quite eventful. It wasn't a good idea to walk on the pavement very much, so Geraldine and I travelled everywhere in a rickshaw. We visited a British club to see a horse-racing event; joined a flower show event, which was spectacular; and toured inside Queen Victoria's Museum, apart from viewing beautiful mosques. It was a great place which we enjoyed. Then Geraldine and I took another train journey, this time for twenty-seven hours, from Calcutta to New Delhi. The train was practically the same set-up as our previous train. The new meals were brought on at nearly every station, and we stopped for collecting and returning used dishes only. So we always had fresh food, and they were always hot meals too. I do remember being given afternoon salads, which were very nice. These train journeys were all spectacular.

In New Delhi, it was freezing cold. It was a modern city, but there was an old part too. Four weeks previous, we had left the sunshine behind, even though it was the Indian winter, which, in comparison, is hotter than an English summer. Fortunately, we had brought our coats, scarves, gloves, and boots to be prepared for this very cold weather.

Each time, we met up with Captain Kiran, although he was working. We three stayed in a very large ornate house in Calcutta which was originally built for an English couple. There was a Chinese cook to make our meals, and since he was the cook for the English couple too before, he knew a few English dishes. But my friends Geraldine and the captain particularly liked the Indian dishes he made specially for them; being Indian, they preferred Indian cuisine. The cook also made meals for the house janitor, who slept in a shed outside.

Also, outside the front gates of this house in Park Road, there was a family living on the floor by a big tree. Often, when we three arrived home in the evening after an event, we had to step over the sleeping people. This big tree was their home.

Everything hung from it—washing pots and pans, even a shiny tin which they used as a mirror. Also, they had a floor cooking range too. In this family, there were the parents, three children, two elder brothers, and a grandma. They were always busy making things and laughing and joking amongst themselves all day.

On the other hand, I would sit indoors, reading a book by the window while looking out at a beautiful large back garden which the janitor would work in every day. In Calcutta, we hadn't reached the cold area. New Delhi, unlike Calcutta, had wide open roads and plenty of buses which were identical to London buses but were much older. Even so, it was a bustling city with high-flying shops and stores. In the centre was the Red Fort, and on the grounds was held a daily laser show. With seats all round, the onlookers listened to galloping horses and Indian girl dancers singing, laughing, and running around, all inside the windows of the Red Fort. On one window, the image of Mahatma Gandhi peered over documents and writing. The whole event was all very realistic, and it was worth a visit to New Delhi just to see this particular show. The Red Fort was an unused prison.

We stayed in a hotel called the Imperial for three weeks. The staff were very honest and helpful; we had to leave all our belongings with them while we went sightseeing. We took a train to Agra, where we stayed for ten days in a Spanish bungalow hotel even though Delhi and Agra were freezing cold. We visited the Taj Mahal, which is the most beautiful building in the world. The train to Agra was a sleeper which took three hours; it was the Taj Express. I saw a few passengers walking around in pyjamas and then putting their seats in sleep mode.

On arriving in Agra, we took an open taxi to find our Spanish hotel, but the journey was very unusual. The area was not commercial at all. There were street traders sitting on the ground on each side of the road. While there were areas along the road on each side with doorways in dusty buildings, there were awnings above that stretched all the way through the whole street. On the awnings sat small monkeys who took great delight in flying over the road from one side to the other. While they were doing their antics, we three got covered in dust; even our driver looked yellow and dusty. Our taxi was covered in the back, with open seating; it had a motorbike engine. Our driver found us a car to use for ten days; he and his brother took turns driving us daily. It was a closed-in car (a Ford).

At the end of our stay, the hotel owner, named Ali, asked me to stay and help him run the hotel. It was a lovely offer which flattered me, but being the mother of two daughters in England, I had to say no. One night, Ali took me to the Taj Mahal to see it in the moonlight. It was beautiful; it looked like see-through marble and opaque icing sugar. It had extraordinary colours, and it was really the only way to truly see the Taj. The whole evening was very romantic.

Geraldine and I visited other sites in Agra. One place was Quata Mar, a tall structure. At this place, I met someone I knew very well—Sir Michael Foot, the English MP. He was with his friend, the chief of police of Delhi. Sir Michael invited us to tea, which brought us together again for the first time since I met him back when I worked for Ernest Marples. Our tea was lovely, and our time together was so memorable.

Geraldine and I went on to visit other areas. Even though it wasn't commercial, there were hidden-away places to see, pointed out to us by the locals, especially artefact shops, where Geraldine bought quite a few keepsakes.

On leaving Agra, which was sad, we took the Taj Express back to New Delhi and stayed two more nights in the Imperial. We both took a train from New Delhi to Bombay, leaving the captain in New Delhi, still working. He never took our train journeys, everywhere. The train journey this time took twenty-five hours; our previous train journeys, although longer, were set in a triangle. It was the same procedure on this train, and again I had the middle bed to sleep on. These beds were so comfortable; I really wished I could take them home.

I just want to mention that on the train lines, during our long journeys, our drivers had a lot to contend with. Every so often, the train stopped to shoo away hogs, who made a practice of setting up home on the line. Sometimes a donkey would walk along in front of the train, and it also had to be shooed away.

Families lived on the platforms. Unfortunately, a lot of families lived on the waterfront in Bombay in canvas tents, but each had free Sky TV and electricity and paid rent to the owner of the canvas tents and sand on the waterfront. These families were often not there in the winter. While there, they worked in houses or just begged; in dense winter, they all went back to their places in the country, where their families back in the country had been growing vegetables to feed everyone in the winter. Usually, in big houses, one family lived together.

CHAPTER TWENTY

GEC and Operation

My time working for GEC lasted eight years, and during this time I had health issues. I was the YTS (Youth Training Scheme) Administrator for five years, and then I was transferred to the Laboratory for three years as Administrator because GEC were joining together with French company Alsthom to form GEC Alsthom to build the Channel Tunnel; it was a real achievement for both countries. My office sometimes housed parts of the tunnel which needed attention. One large slab was letting in water. My engineers took this to the stresses and strain machine to be tested and recalibrated. We obviously got it right because the Channel Tunnel doesn't let water in.

I feel proud to have been part of the administration in the building of the Channel Tunnel – it being such a historic achievement.

This appointment in the GEC Laboratory was quite an exciting time for me – also it was the last job in my working life.

During my time at GEC, I had different operations. One was a bladder repair, which was a sensitive operation, causing me to take four months off work. After three months, GEC sent me away to Hampsfield House, Grange-Over-Sands, to their company convalescent home, which they shared with British Aerospace. The house was so grand; it was like a small royal palace. It was absolutely beautiful. The grounds were magnificent. When I returned to Hampsfield House recently, I was upset to see it is now an apartment complex. I suppose the upkeep was too expensive, but I thought, *What a shame.*

I left GEC in 1994, having been made redundant. This did not upset me because I was looking forward to lying in bed instead of rushing out of the house at 7 a.m. in all kinds of weather to begin work at 8 a.m. I was the only Administrator. I never left work until well after 7 p.m. I was always the last to leave. As I had no help, it was a tough job, and everything had to be so precise. Apart from that, I was sorry to leave. Even so, I now had new paths to find.

CHAPTER TWENTY-ONE

After Studies and Own Businesses (1985)

Unfortunately, I lost my lovely mum. She went to join my dad in March 1984. During the summer, I worked for Mr Jeffrey Thompson, owner of Blackpool Pleasure Beach. At first, I was secretary to the director of Construction and Engineering and the director of Operations. Both eventually left, so for a short while, I was transferred to the main office. Mr Thompson used to go to Myrtle Beach in South Carolina, USA; he had a pleasure beach there. I often went there because my family had a timeshare in that area. It was a very good complex. Mr Thompson was a kind man and worked very hard. Unfortunately, he died, leaving Pleasure Beach in the capable hands of his daughter.

As I was still living in Graham's and my little house, it became necessary for me to move because the house had subsidence. Eventually, the insurance company paid me out to enable me to rebuy, which I did, but this time I bought a converted first-floor apartment in a large two-fronted Edwardian house. The house was very grand, and it was a joy living in it. This happened in August 1985.

In October 1985, I visited Mrs Tunstall, a medium who lived in Blackpool, for a spiritual reading. This was after my businesses failed. I was without work because I no longer worked for Pleasure Beach; most parts shut in the winter, while the separate ice show keeps going. Mrs Tunstall told me I was with dark people and that I was going over water, but it was strange because I was also in a factory. She was completely right too.

As it happened, my name was with a job centre. I was sent for and told to go to GEC Preston for an interview. Carrying out their wishes, I joined others in applying for a lone vacancy and took several tests. These tests were all coded, and when the judging committee segregated them (like a competition), mine came first out of fifteen contestants. So I was offered a job as the administrator of the training scheme known as YTS. It was for young students of sixteen to eighteen years old without work who did not want to attend college, and it covered hairdressing, mechanical work, catering, and organisation. Students were married in with sponsors already in business. YTS paid the students to learn and gave the sponsors a grant to take on the students.

However, after this interview and job offer, I had a telephone call from the Midland Bank manager. 'Come into the branch for a chat.' This was not my bank. I went to the interview and was told that my friend from India was inviting me to go over to (then) Bombay on December 24 for two months. I seem to remember that the airfare was paid. The reason for this was that my friend and his family had often stayed at my place over the years, and this visit was a present. In fact, my friend had had his five-week honeymoon at my place. He was the captain of a P & O ship and had needed to do a £3,000 course at Nautical College, Fleetwood. He now has two shipping companies and two at-sea cargo ships. Since then, I have often stayed over, for two months each time.

I phoned GEC to say I wouldn't be able to take the administrator's position, but I was asked to talk about it over lunch, which I did. I explained my change of mind. It was decided I would begin work at once, because the appointment was brand new, and if I set up the new office with a new filing system intact and with records set up, I could have two months off. So this appointment began with no time for me to go home and change, and even no papers to investigate, which was the usual practice for a new employee. When beginning a new job, these papers should be seen. I mentioned this and was told 'We do not need yours. You have signed the Official Secrets Act so many times, and your curriculum vitae tells us all we want to know about you.'

GEC paid me for two weeks instead of having me wait a month, then for another two months at the end of the two weeks, saying, 'It is just one month that you will not receive pay, and we will see you after Christmas when you return on February 4.' I told a colleague about the arrangement, and they told me that GEC was being more than fair and wished me luck.

It was in this job that stipulated I had to have the City and Guilds teacher training certificate, because I was teaching students office procedures when students came to me between jobs they had finished with their sponsor. It was the Manpower Services Commission who paid for my evening college fees. I also had to spend one afternoon every week teaching students communication at Tuson College, Fulwood.

CHAPTER TWENTY-TWO

Redundancy

1994

In 1994 I was actually made redundant. The Channel Tunnel had now been built, and the firm was becoming smaller. The YTS had shrunk too, and I think its name had also changed. The redundancy was an unusual one. A lot of employees were made redundant—the director of resources, the general manager and his secretary, the personnel manager, and others of note. But when they were issued redundancy, they were each at once escorted off the premises, followed by the safety officer, named Reg. With their private belongings, they were taken to the car park. It must have been terribly embarrassing to have been made to leave a firm that way.

I was called into the wages department, where my boss, Keith D., was sitting. Then I was told that I was being made redundant but was being given six months' notice and that I could leave at any time within that period, with redundancy pay. Before, in the laboratory, there were twenty-two engineers, my boss, and his assistant. They were both transferred to another section. Five engineers left of their own accord, and other engineers were transferred. With only a few in the office left, there was a lot of clearing-up work to do, so my remaining months were indeed very busy. However, I did leave before the six months were up. My leaving was quite natural; I very tearfully collected the small redundancy pay. I was even given extra six weeks' holiday money, which helped me financially.

I said goodbye to friends round the factory and those left at work still. In fact, this took me all day. Realising that this was a sad occasion, it made me feel sad too. It was winter, and my first morning at home, I sniffed out of the window at quarter to seven and said to myself, 'Whey hey,' and jumped back in bed.

CHAPTER TWENTY-THREE

All's Well

After flying high for most of my life and overcoming every obstacle, it was a surprise when I discovered a lump growing at the top of my left leg. I watched this lump grow, and so did my doctors. But one morning I woke up to find that this well-looked-at lump had split into two. I thought, *That's not right*. So at 8.30 in the morning, I hightailed straight to my doctor and sat on the steps until surgery opened. Of course, when staff arrived, I was told 'You must have an appointment', but I was saved by my doctor, who took me straight in.

My doctor was also puzzled as to why the lump had split into two, and he immediately phoned my surgeon at Royal Preston Hospital, Lancashire, who asked me to come down. So I did. At the hospital that same afternoon, I was immediately seen to by an in-house surgeon who took the offending split lump away, leaving me with stitches and a complaint that lumps were deep and wide.

Anyway, three days later, my surgeon phoned to tell me to come back and bring a family member, which, of course, I did. The only one available was my grandson. I was told I had cancer. There was not too much explanation, but they asked if I could come back tomorrow with my daughter who lived near me at the time. The next day, at the hospital, it was explained that I had melanoma, brought about by me having got too much sun when I was a small child. Of course, I didn't remember that, only that there were times when I was covered in camomile lotion-type white powder; I even remembered my mum saying, 'You've been burned by the sun.' But I had only been little then.

A few days later, my daughter came to visit me with her five children. Looking back, I think they all visited because they were worried for me; they thought I was going to pop off there and then. Of course, no such thing happened. While at the time I was perplexed as to how this happened, it didn't worry me. At the hospital, melanoma was explained in more detail, and I was given more details and was told to be in the backup cancer department, headed by a young lady and her assistant, who were both on call twenty-four hours a day to answer any questions phoned in.

First off for me was a scheduled head-to-toe MRI scan, after which was the removal of one of my big toenails; the findings were negative. The scan showed no other abnormalities. Up till then, my imagination had run riot. My first thoughts were that I could go look for a boxer puppy; having had two boxer dogs, I am a fan of them. I thought I was going to undergo a lot of treatments, like chemotherapy or radiotherapy, and was going to lose my hair, but I did not care. I thought my puppy and I could have so much fun together. I also refused chemo.

But melanoma is a skin cancer. I am now in remission. I've had lumps taken out twice. One was taken from the top of my nose, which only left a redness; nothing else was detected. My hospital surgeon sends for me every few months to arrange scans. So far, I have had two PET scans and two CT scans, each one from head to toe. Nothing has been detected, but if ever, my surgeon will pounce. Also, I had neck operations to take lumps away.

I am so lucky to be looked after so well in our great country, with national healthcare being freely available. I feel well knowing that I am so well-cared-for here in jolly UK.

CHAPTER TWENTY-FOUR

Health

At the beginning of being diagnosed with cancer, I happened to be writing emails on my iPad when a clip came on-screen. 'Do you know your blood type? Do you eat according to it?' This clip was from a doctor in China. Because it interrupted me, I decided to find out. It took me two months to find out. Strangely, my surgeon hadn't any knowledge, but after many setbacks, I eventually found out that my blood type is rhesus positive, group A. I was advised to be vegetarian, wheat-free, and soy-free. Also, all sugar types had to be eliminated, like sugar and syrups. I could eat fowl and fish, but not sea bass, which I used to like.

My diet before this revelation wasn't a bad one; I did not ever eat junk food. Nevertheless, for the past fifty years at least, I had been subject to being sick at night four times a week and had heartburn six times a week every night. I thought everyone had heartburn. I always thought the reason I was sick was that I was born without a lining in my stomach and my mother had made an artificial one by adding the white of an egg to a baby bottle for two years. But as it happened, my beliefs were untrue. Since the day I read the plan, I changed my diet, and to this day, I have not had heartburn at all and have only undergone sickness twice. Once was my own fault; I cheated. The other time was because the cream in a hotel was off, and a few customers didn't feel well either.

There is no chance that I will not follow my eating plan. My diet is extremely healthy, and I do Nutribullet juicing nearly every morning using fresh fruits and green vegetables. Also, of course, it is well known that glucose and sugar feed cancer cells, so with me having hardly any sugar, the cancer cells have withered. Now I have no cancer and am termed as being in remission.

CHAPTER TWENTY-FIVE

Healthy Changes

From 1994 to 2000, I underwent a few operations, which kept me in hospital a lot. One operation, a thyroidectomy in Lytham Hospital, was a different kind of experience. It was then that I lost my operative singing voice. As I was second soprano in a large local choir, Lytham St Anne's Choral Society, it was a really upsetting blow for me. I had the operation the same week as lovely actress Julie Andrews, and her surgeon couldn't save her beautiful voice either. She was very well known for her role as the nun in the famous film *The Sound of Music*. Julie's surgeon explained to millions of upset viewers exactly why Julie's singing voice was destroyed in her thyroidectomy.

While I was in hospital for over two weeks, my surgeon came to talk to me. 'I have good news and bad news. The good news is, you can go home this afternoon, but the bad news is, you have to be a day patient for a further week.' I said, 'Thank you, but you have it the wrong way round. I don't want to leave this afternoon. I would rather stay and not be a day patient, because I would already be here.' Still being cheeky, that's what I said. The ward sister said, 'What do you think we are, a Butlins holiday camp?' They all stalked off.

Whenever I was in hospital, I always mentioned to the staff, 'Don't wake me up for an early morning cup of tea, and if breakfast is early, please leave me asleep.' I was never woken up. However, after the ward party had left me to pack my things to go home, the ward sister came back to me with a cup of tea in hand. She was smiling. 'Well, Joanne,' she said, 'you can stay for another ten days, but you have to do a task for us.' Taking the cup of tea and being grateful, I asked, 'What is this task?' The sister said, 'Go round with the orderly with the trolley of early morning cups of tea and give patients a cup of tea.' I replied, 'Really? Are you serious?' She said, 'Yes, because we are very short-staffed, and without you helping, no one will have their early morning teas. Oh, and also, you will have your meals with the staff instead of being served in bed by the trolley service.'

I lived alone and didn't look forward to going home and then having to go back every day as an outpatient, so of course, I said yes, biting my tongue. Uggggh, I had to wake up early every morning. But, of course, I did it, and it worked out very well. I even extended my help with the afternoon tea trolley as well, as I was getting better the whole time.

CHAPTER TWENTY-SIX

From Year 2000

During the time of the millennium, there was much speculation as to what might happen in the eye of the millennium. Governments and business premises donated a lot of money to technology. It was just an ordinary change of date, but even so, it was good to be sceptical and to put into practice the new packages in case something went wrong.

Since the year 2000, quite a lot of events have taken place. Apart from my undergoing operations, there were many holidays, particularly several months in Bombay (now known as Mumbai) and several months at many different times in Pennsylvania, USA, staying with my daughter Sandralee and her family—her husband, Jeff; two daughters, Sarah and Suzannah; and a son, Jed. Now Sarah has a two-year-old daughter and a baby girl of a few months old.

My daughter Karen has five children, and many weekends were taken up with me childminding. All the while, Karen was singing in hotels and clubs, which was a good way to help pay her household bills. Karen's children were her eldest son, Craig; his sister, Stephanie; and his brother, Philip, followed a few years later by a brother and sister, Alexander and Sally.

Fortunately, all my grandchildren are delightful and a pleasure to be with. My grandson Philip has a lovely partner, Siobhan, who is adorable, and they have a daughter, age seven. My other grandson Craig also has a partner, Leighan, who is a very jolly young lady. They have a four-year-old son and twins, a boy and a girl, now one year old.

I adore my friends in Mumbai too. Living on my own causes me no problems; I have wonderful friends: Beverley, my ex-sister-in-law; June and Ray; Arlene; Audrey; and later Kathy. I also would not forget my good friends Brian, Mary, and Maxine from the Seventh-Day Adventist Church, which I have been a member of for many years. There is also my good neighbour Rochelle and her family, Dr Christine and Gillian E., Pat, and my dear friend Alan Gill.

Of course, I could go on saying the names of everyone I enjoy spending company with, but I hope they know who I mean even if their name isn't here. Before, it was difficult for me to go through life with no friends. Also, I often see my school friend Duggie Falk, who lives in Worthing, Surrey. We often go on holidays, which is always good fun.

CHAPTER TWENTY-SEVEN

My Girls

Throughout the years, my girls, Karen Jane and Sandralee, have each grown up to be the finest of the fine. Now both in their fifties, both have shown so much talent. Both attended college, gaining their qualifications.

Karen went to art college for five years, studying fine art, graphic design, and photography. Being a high achiever, she became an expert in all these subjects. She uses all these skills in her current work as a promoter in the entertainment business, producing her own posters for shows and writing her own reports for newspapers. Apart from this, she is also a brilliant artist; her paintings are exceptional, good, and well sought after. Karen lives in Cyprus; she has been married twice and has five children and now four grandchildren.

After the traumatic beginnings in her father's life and my life, she settled down and has achieved much to her advantage to give her a bright future. Karen also has a very good singing voice and often entertains in shows of her own in Cyprus. Her family and I visit her often.

Sandralee, on the other hand, showed talent in organisation and languages, which she has used all her working life. She speaks several languages, and after a few years in marketing, travelling around the world, she now teaches languages in a school in the USA. Her students all love her. Sandralee put a lot of effort into studying and gained two degrees, a masters and a principalship. She met her husband while working in Germany, and she now lives in the USA. She has three children and now two grandchildren. Sandralee lives within the Amish community in Pennsylvania, in a beautiful scenic area which she calls 'the boonies'. It is a forty-five-minute car ride to the nearest shopping precinct, which is at Erie.

I often think that having two such talented daughters is my greatest achievement.

CHAPTER TWENTY-EIGHT

Interests and Hobbies

It is always a pleasure to be involved in hobbies and entertainment. Fortunately, from birth, I have always loved music, singing, and let's not forget dancing (stage and ballroom). As a little girl, I was a Terry baby. Later, I was one of the Terry juveniles, which were the younger groups of the older Tiller Girls, wearing top hats, carrying canes, and kicking out our legs together in a long row. Our classes were in Leicester Square. My love of ballet has continued throughout. As Terry juveniles, we were treated to afternoon tea by Margot Fonteyn and Robert Helpmann. They were so lovely. It's a memory which I have always treasured.

After I was a Tiller Girl for a short time, the group was disbanded in England. They were transferred to Radio City in New York, and their name was changed to the Rockets; they still perform today, on the stage, before the showing of an epic film. All other girls near 6' tall were sent to Paris and became known as the Bluebell Girls. They were mostly in Moulin Rouge in Paris. Of course, I was not allowed to go to New York because I still had heart trouble and had to be near my doctors in England. Even kicking high was not a good idea.

During my show life, I was in many pantomimes. In my last pantomime at Wimbledon Theatre, I was a cherry tree in their production of *Sinbad the Sailor*, with comedian Sid Field. I was not allowed to dance too much, but there was a scene where a decoration was needed; I fitted the bill.

Also, I enjoyed singing; I had a high-pitched voice. This took me into many choirs. This is the time to tell that I also have an allotment where I grow my own vegetables. Fortunately, I love jazz, rap, heavy music, pop songs, ballads, and operas; I like watching ballet, and I have a great love for all classical music. My favourite orchestra conductor is André Rieu, who has an extraordinary number of talented musicians. His orchestra plays the most wonderful Viennese waltzes. André's 2009 concert in London is worth seeing on TV time and time again (which I have).

Throughout my life, there have been and there still are very talented singers: Frank Sinatra, Pavarotti, Russell Watson, and Jose Ferrera, to name a few. I am even a fan of Matt Cardle, who won *The X Factor* in 2010. I also enjoy country music and dancing to country and Western music too, wearing large dresses, as seen in the film *Gone with the Wind*. Even so, following the Bolshoi Ballet performances takes up a lot of my time.

Also, I still enjoy drawing and painting, and to this end, I do attend a local church with a few friends every week to paint our own pictures. There is no teacher; to meet for relaxation is good fun. A lot of my time is also spent trying to help others. Previously, for twenty-five years, I was the lady almoner for the conservative club in St Anne's, Lancashire, my home town. I used to visit members in hospital, with follow-ups at home. Unfortunately, the club closed in 2016. Recently, my friend June mentioned that she and her husband thought I was Florence Nightingale. I enjoy helping others and always will. My love of being a multitasker still continues, with me being on quite a few committees and organising different events in different societies.

CHAPTER TWENTY-NINE

Blackpool Victoria Hospital

During my times as Lady Almoner for the Conservative Club for 25 years in St Annes, one 2017 hospital visit involved me staying in hospital for 31 hours. The patient's nieces lived near Liverpool and his sister lived in the USA. The nurses persuaded me to remain until we lost our friend - I was given carte blanche to use staff kitchens for coffee or tea or sandwiches, even though they brought me all my meals.

At 1.30 in the morning the Matron of Blackpool Victoria Hospital found me - handed me Mr Cullen's address book - a pile of cards and asked me to write to everyone in book to give sad news of James Cullen's passing - after which to give all back to her to be franked and posted.

I eventually arrived back indoors at 2.30am, quite exhausted from all those hours not sleeping.

The reason for relating above is to acknowledge how caring the Staff are in Blackpool hospital - in such times - as this grave need.

CHAPTER THIRTY

Just Good Friends

As I had lost my memory a little and belonged to the Lytham Hospital Memory Clinic, it was eventually decided that I be transferred to a memory social group in a church across the road. This group was very successful for a few years, and the staff running the group were unfortunately pulled out by the NHS due to lack of funds.

However, that week, I was sent to a hotel in St Anne's to join a meeting to set up a 'help each other' group. But this group never materialised. Instead, on my entering the hotel, I saw that the person sitting inside was my ex-sister-in-law, Beverley, Graham's sister. It was such a pleasure to see her. Beverley wanted to set up a 'lonely people' group, so of course, I joined in.

The group began with four of us, but after nearly six years, it has grown to hundreds. The name of our group is Just Good Friends. I took on the role of group event organiser and club photographer. My iPad takes brilliant pictures so very clearly. In this capacity, the members have had a chance to visit many places; we even took a trip to Wales, visiting Llandudno.

Last year, a few of us spent time rehearsing with *Britain's Got Talent*'s Diversity. This was quite exciting, and the result was a TV show featuring Beverley to thank her for her achievement in bringing so many lonely local people together every day of the week to join so many activities.

This is my story now, right up to this date. It is a pleasure to continue in daily events with so many lovely, lovely friends and a wonderful family (two daughters, eight grandchildren, six great-grandchildren, and all their spouses/partners).

1 January 2018. Happy New Year!
My friends.

Printed in the United States
By Bookmasters